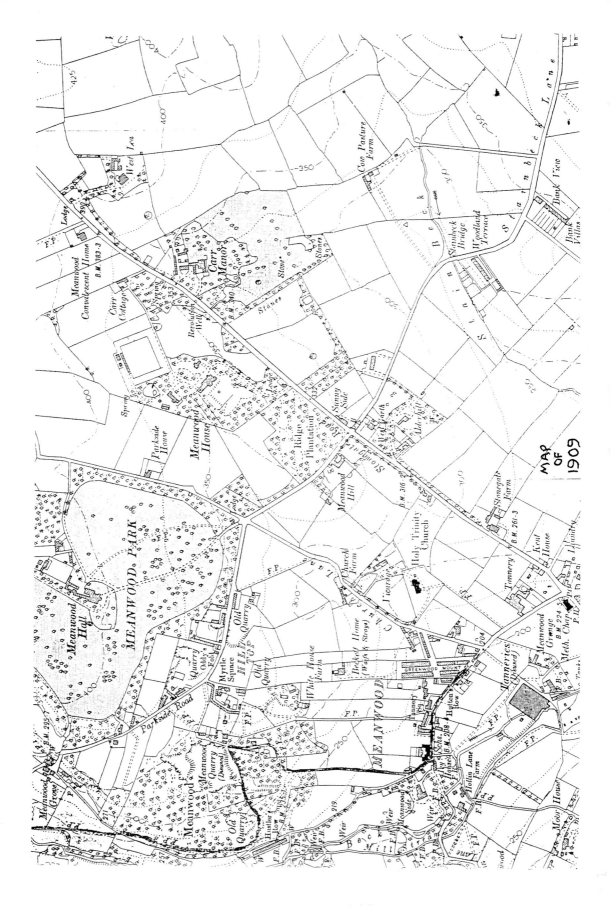

MAP OF 1909

THE MEANWOOD VILLAGE ASSOCIATION PRESENTS

MEANWOOD
IN
PICTURES

DOREEN WOOD, one of the founders of the Association in 1972 and tireless worker ever since. She served as Secretary in the early years and is currently Vice Chairman. She is pictured here with her beloved cine film equipment. She has made many films, often featuring Meanwood, and won various awards.

(Photograph courtesy of *Yorkshire Post* Newspapers)

VOLUME 4 — 2001 to 2012

Compiled by
PETER BEWELL

Assisted by
ANNE BURGESS, BRYN EVANS and DOREEN WOOD

Published by
M.V.A. Publications

95 Green Road
Meanwood
Leeds LS6 4LE

First published 2012

ISBN 978 0 9547946 4 4

Printed and bound by
Smith Settle Printing and Bookbinding Ltd
Gateway Drive, Yeadon, West Yorkshire LS19 7XY

ACKNOWLEDGEMENTS

Sincere thanks to all who have contributed in any way to the production of this volume, which will hopefully show future generations what Meanwood was like in the first decade of the 21st century.

CONTENTS

In this volume we have divided the contents into a number of sections as follows.

MEANWOOD IN PICTURES

"The Village within a city"

How time flies! It does not seem long since I was writing the foreword for Volume 3, but there have been many changes since that special Millennium year and we have tried to illustrate them here.

The most notable changes have occurred in the centre of our village in the area known to the older generation as "The Terminus" (dating back to the days of the trams when they terminated at the crossroads of Meanwood Road and Stonegate Road).

The most notable change was the building of the large Waitrose supermarket in 2010. This site has seen many changes over the years. Originally it was a market garden managed by the aptly named Mr Groundwell, and then in 1922 the Capitol Parade was built which consisted of the Capitol Cinema and Ballroom and a parade of shops.

This was demolished, and Meanwood's first supermarket was built in 1981. The development also included a few shops and the Yorkshire Bank. The supermarket was originally G.T. Smith but later it became the Co-op.

In 2010 all this was demolished and the big Waitrose store constructed and opened on 30th September.

The other big project was the demolition of the Beckett's pub in 2007 and the erection of a building consisting of 24 flats over several shops and a wine bar called "East of Arcadia".

The Meanwood Village Association was pleased to be involved in both these schemes at the planning stages, and had a number of meetings with management and their architects.

There is no doubt that these schemes have 'lifted' the profile of Meanwood.

On April 22nd 2011 a full page article appeared in *The Times* newspaper headed "The Waitrose effect" outlining the many benefits that occur in an area when a Waitrose store is opened. This is easily seen by the build up of traffic and customers flooding in from other areas.

Another noticeable feature in Meanwood is the large increase in houses being extended. Instead of moving to larger premises residents are resorting to utilising roof spaces, building over garages, and extending in various ways.

Solar panels have also been installed on a number of houses.

In the last couple of years there has also been a noticeable change in all the street lighting with tall metal standards replacing the smaller ones which have been around since the demise of the old gas lamps many years ago.

During 2010 and 2011 the Health Centre was extensively enlarged and modernised.

Meanwood now has its own World Champion! Claire O'Hara won the world squirt boating title in 2009 and then crowned it by winning the world title for freestyle kayaking in 2011. If you are wondering what a squirt boat is, it is a small kayak in which the competitor has to perform all sorts of acrobatic feats in a fast flowing river.

Well done Claire!

Peter Bewell
March 2012

*** We are always pleased to receive photographs, both old and new, to add to our collection. You can either donate them or lend them to us for copying.

Please give dates, names, and locations if at all possible. Just contact any of the officers listed on the backpage. Thank you.

Prince Charles on a visit to the Meanwood Valley Urban Farm in 2002.

ARTHUR HOPWOOD, a well known and respected Meanwood historian who died in 2008 at the age of 86. He was a staunch Methodist and was involved in all aspects of the church. On his return from war service in 1946 he became the assistant Scoutmaster and steadily rose up the ranks to District Commissioner for N.W. Leeds and received the 'Silver Wolf' at a ceremony at Windsor Castle. Together with his friend Fred Casperson he wrote the 'Meanwood' history book published in 1986. It is still selling today and sales exceed 4,000 copies.

Bentley Lane School

Children leaving the Methodist Church after farewell service.

Demolition begins in September 2009

Demolition in full swing. A sad day for many who attended the school which was built in the 1920s.

In 2009 an inter-generation party was held at Meanwood C.of E. Primary School where the older generation enjoyed mixing with the children, playing games and chatting about how things were in their days, and being served tea.

Children enjoying a ballet class held in the School Hall.

Photograph courtesy of *Yorkshire Post* Newspapers.

It was a sad day on the 26th January 2010 when the Yorkshire Bank closed its doors for the last time, and all the customer accounts were transferred to the Headingley branch.

This was just before the demolition men moved in prior to the building of the new Waitrose.

A group of M.V.A. members at Roy Hall's 60th birthday celebrations.
Roy is the Chairman of the M.V.A. Committee.

A large group of M.V.A. members assembling for the annual Easter Tuesday walk around
Meanwood in 2005.

*Jackie Brewer, a long serving
member of the M.V.A.*

*Elaine, the Park Ranger, and Chris Needham,
clearing the pond.*

*Guests at the Meanwood Institute celebrating M.V.A. Vice Chairman Doreen Wood's 90th birthday and
the Chairman Roy Hall and his wife Barbara's 40th wedding anniversary.*

The old tannery, just off Monkbridge Road, which has been converted into flats.

Meanwood Hall, which dates back to 1762, is situated in the centre of the Woodlea estate, and is also being converted into flats.

An extension to the front of the Aldi store in 2008.

Originally the first Methodist Chapel in Meanwood. Later it became a laundry, a builders merchant's, and then Acorn Glass.

In 2005/6 it was converted into dwellings.

The shops and businesses at the bottom of Stonegate Road.

Steven and Pepi in the FOBI shop selling books for the M.V.A.

Tony Taylor and Pete Spedding with the Men's Society bowls trophy for 2011

In 2011 the Methodist Church celebrated 200 years of Methodism in Meanwood with a special service in September led by a former minister, The Revd Alan Powers. He came along with his Puppet and gave a fascinating sermon.

At the beginning of the 2nd world war two young girls were evacuated from Leeds to Ilkley and were cared for by the same family, and they became close friends. They were Lucy Preston and Dorothy Williamson. They then lost touch with each other for over 60 years until in 2005 they were reunited through a researcher Alan Magson and the magic of the internet. Dorothy is seen on the right of the picture.

(Photograph courtesy of *Yorkshire Post* Newspapers)

The winter of 2010/11 was very severe and here in December we see the frozen beck.

The beck in spate.

A winter wonderland. The frozen pond in the park in January2001.

A fisherman tries his luck on a sunny cold day in February 2003.

Colin Taylor, games organiser.

Phil Chilvers (Chapel) and
Richard Wiggen (Church).

TSUNAMI

Following the disastrous Tsunami in Sri Lanka on
Boxing Day 2004 Shirley Barber, Kay Smithson
and Christine Bewell rapidly organised a fund
raising day on January 2nd at the Institute, with
games, raffle, tombola and a donation box, and
raised over £4,000.

This was sent immediately to the National Appeal
and over the next few weeks other events were
arranged and more money raised which was sent
via the Bishop of Ripon and Leeds to the Bishop of
Colombo in Sri Lanka.

It was used for immediate relief to the devastated
communities for buying new fishing boats and
nets.

Richard Wiggen, with Alan and Dorothy Menzies.

Beverley Fox, Janet Turner, and Janet Matthews.

Matthew Laurillard receiving a raffle prize.

Elated Elaine!

Bryn Evans.

Jane Charlesworth.

Wendy Pinder.

Rita Durrant.

Alan Corners and Arthur Barber.

Margaret Jackson doing the big count up.

The Co-op in January 2010 just prior to demolition.

December 2009. They certainly were !

Co-op demolition in full swing in March 2010.

Clearing rubble, and the start of new drainage system.

TEA & CHAT

John Wallace the ukulele man.

Three times a year the committee of the Meanwood Institute invite about 35 elderly (or housebound) local residents to Sunday afternoon tea, with some entertainment. Transport is provided where needed. Always much appreciated.

Three Guests obviously enjoying it. Walter Hall, Victor Clough and Mike Osborne in 2004.

At Christmas time Santa always manages to fit in a visit and here he is with Rose Kelly and Edith Addy in 2007.

Entertainment from the Church Drama Group in 2008.

The Choir from Meanwood C. of E. Primary School Green Road in 2004.

CHURCH IMPROVEMENTS

During 2006 a number of projects were carried out at the Church. New paths were laid, entrance steps built, new toilets created and trees trimmed.

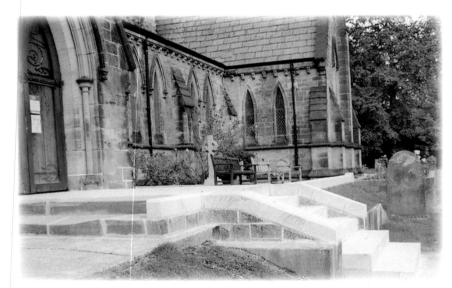

On the left, Alan Smith, Chris Needham, and Keith Slaney and on the right Lesley Slaney, Francis Needham and Carol Smith.

Roy Hall on the left and Barbara Hall front right, with Iain Burgess, and Sylvia Evans.

CELEBRATIONS

In August 2010 a party took place at the Institute to celebrate two special events. The 40th wedding anniversary of the M.V.A. Chairman Roy Hall and his wife Barbara, and the 90th birthday of the Deputy Chairman, Doreen Wood. Both Doreen and Roy have been stalwarts of the Association for many years.

Doreen, the Birthday Girl with her bouquet.

Doreen with her friends Edna Lolley, on left and Margaret Rolls, on right.

Site clearance and piling in progress, July 2007.

THE BECKETTS

There have been a number of
buildings on this site over the years.
In 2007 the old pub was demolished
and a new building erected. This
consisted of some shop units and a
wine bar at street level with 24 flats
above.

*Construction in progress in
November 2007.*

The main structure almost complete.

An interesting view from the top flat looking up Stonegate Road in October 2008.

From the same flat, a colourful scene looking westwards towards the old tannery.

32

Lady helpers at the Chapel luncheon club with Christine Bewell who had run it for 27 years. Dorothy Williamson, Lily Slade, Dorothy Carrol, Christine Bewell, Doris Spence and Brenda Binge.

Chapel Youth Club reunion in 2006. Christine Bewell, Pat Jackson, Pauline Micklethwaite, Pauline Lalley, Mike Lalley and Irene Holstead.

The same reunion.

Gordon Rowling, Terry Richardson, and Brian Horsey at the 2006 reunion.

Another reunion, this time in 2008. On the left from front Pauline and Mike Lalley, Gay Hall, and Eileen Barratt and on the right from front Christine Bewell, Jack and June Collinson, Robert and Betty Pattinson.

WOW! Parkside Allotments Flower and Vegetable show at the Parochial Hall in August 2008.

The same show a year later with Tony Taylor presenting a bouquet to Councillor Brenda Lancaster.

A prize winning gladiolus, one of many wonderful flowers on show.

A change of venue now with Joe Maiden judging at the Hollin Lane Allotments show.

Claire O'Hara, World Champion on the water.

Sign on the side of her van.

*Outside the Institute in 2009 at a fund raising day letting the little ones
have a go in her squirt boats.*

Jubilation, A GOLD MEDAL !

Peter Bewell, President of the Meanwood Village Association presenting Claire with a cheque to help her buy a new kayak.

HOUSE EXTENSIONS

Three roof extensions creating extra bedrooms.

Another increasingly common feature in 2011 was the installation of domestic solar panels.

A bungalow seen here with a major extension.

Another style of roof extension.

Good use of roof space.

A major extension.

Carol singers from Meanwood C. of E. Primary School outside Waitrose on November 23rd 2011 prior to the Christmas street lights being switched on.

More singers.

Brenda Lancaster, who served Meanwood well during her years as a Councillor.
(Photograph courtesy of *Yorkshire Post* Newspapers)

MEDICAL CENTRE

During 2011 the Meanwood Health Centre at the top of Meanwood Road underwent extensive renovations and extensions.

The modernised waiting room, with the beautiful woodland scene on the wall, and the new seating.

MEANWOOD health centre

The bright new outside sign.

Podiatry 1 - 2
Multi-Function Room
Soft Consulting Rooms 1 - 4
Speech & Language Therapy →

← Podiatry 3 / Clinical Room 1
Toilets

One of several signs indicating the many rooms.

THE URBAN FARM

Sue Reddington, the farm director greeting Prince Charles on his visit to the Meanwood Valley Urban Farm in 2002.

Children with their greetings banner.

Prince Charles talking to an excited group of children.
(Photograph courtesy of *Yorkshire Post* Newspapers)

The Prince chatting to the footballers.

A little lad all dressed up for the occasion.

THE MEANWOOD MONSOON

On the 25th June 2007 torrential rains hit the valley and the beck burst its banks resulting in flooding in various places. The Millside building was seriously affected and all the residents had to be evacuated.

A rather frightened lady being rescued on a tea trolley!

Another lady making the trip to safety.

Another resident being walked through the flood.

Flooded cars.

A rescue boat arrived.

The evacuees were transferred to the Methodist Church schoolroom and given blankets and hot drinks before being taken to other hospital units. Thankfully nobody was hurt.

SHOPS

Shops at the top of Meanwood Road.

Shops (and forecourt) at the bottom of Stonegate Road.

At the corner of Stonegate Road and Green Road.

Shops at the bottom of Stonegate Road.

The Green Road shopping precinct.

Shops at the top of Meanwood Road.

INTER-GENERATION PARTY

The inter-generation parties held at Meanwood C. of E. Primary School are very popular indeed, and both generations enjoy the opportunity to have a good chat.

Playing a game with Aunty Jennie.

Sandra and Brian Glassby with three of the girls.

The audience enjoying a concert.

Obviously enjoying it all.

Time for refreshments.

Who is enjoying it most?

Two Meanwood brothers, Robert and Brian Wheatley decided it was time to sort out the badly neglected spring and trough on 'Dunny Hill' so, in 2005, they did just that.

In 2004 the dry stone wall on Parkside Road near the cricket field was badly in need of repair, so Cynthia Ruston, a local resident, applied for, and received, a grant from the local Heritage Initiative which enabled the wall to be rebuilt by professional dry stone wallers.

The stone marking their efforts.

SIGNS

A sign familiar to the older generation. It is in the Tramway Museum in Derbyshire.

The sign at the entrance to the North Side retail park at the bottom of Stonegate Road.

The very colourful sign outside the school near Meanwoodside Park.

Dear God,
Thank you for today in school
and for all the opportunities for
playing and learning. Thank you
for the happiness that friends
and family bring, and keep us
safe through the night.

Amen

An emotive sign on a wall inside the school.

PARTY IN THE PARK

Several local churches organised a party in the park in July 2011 which proved very successful with all sorts of entertainments and refreshments.

Having a shot at the coconut shy.

Kite making with Supo Ogunyinka, who is the Reader at Holy Trinity Church.

Bouncing the parachute.

The balloon man on his stilts.

The little drummer boy.

The ever popular face painting.

More enthusiastic drumming.

The Cedar Room at the rear of the Methodist Church was built in 1973, but it had to be demolished in 2010 to make way for the Waitrose development.

The rather forlorn scene after its removal.

The new paving to the war memorial on Green Road after the area had been cleared by volunteers. The memorial was built to commemorate the casualties in the battle of the Somme in World War One.

The corner shop at the bottom of Greenwood Mount that was occupied by the Co-op for many years before it became offices for the Fish Fryers Federation.

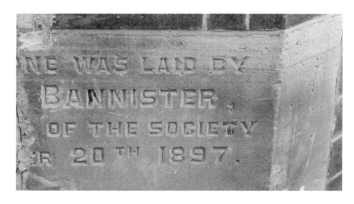

The foundation stone on the above shop, (now plastered over).

Every year in Meanwood there is a Shoebox Appeal. People are requested to fill a box with presents for children. The boxes are then collected and sent off to Eastern Europe and distributed amongst deprived children. Here we see The Vicar, Richard Wiggen receiving some of the boxes in 2006.

Howard Naylor playing the Last Post at the Remembrance Service in 2008.

Kathryn Wiggen enjoying a joke with The Bishop of Knaresborough, James Bell, after a confirmation service in the church in 2005.

Newly appointed clergy in 2008. Rupert Weekes the new Methodist Minister with his wife Esme, and Chris Orme, the Priest in Charge at Holy Trinity Church, and his wife Sarah.

Setting up the 'Little Mice' crib in church in 2005.

Waiting their turn to perform.

One of the shepherds.

Two of the kings.

Sandra Glassby with the Little Mice in 2005.

A wine tasting evening in the Parochial Hall laid on by Waitrose in 2011. Chris Needham, Kevin Wheeler, Jackie Brewer, Sheila Stevenson, Iain Burgess, Anne Burgess and Frances Needham.

WINTER WONDERLAND 2010

The winters of 2010 and 2011 were exceptionally severe, causing all sorts of problems for people, but they also created some spectacular 'Winter Wonderland' scenes, some of which are shown here.

One of the annual Animal Services in the church which were enjoyed by young and old. Here in 2005 is Richard Wiggen with two little girls and their pet dog.

A little girl with her rather fierce looking cat.

Everyone making friends!

First time in church for a lion.

Excited girl and dog.

Feeding time.

Two happy little chaps arriving with their dog.

REDEDICATION OF WAR MEMORIAL

In 2009 the war memorial at the bottom of Memorial Drive underwent a refurbishment, and there was a service of re-dedication in December.

A blessing from the Bishop of Knaresborough.

The service was honoured by the presence of the Lord Mayor, Councillor Judith Elliot.

A veteran, having just laid a wreath, flanked by the Royal British Legion standard bearers.

The Lord Mayor, the Bishop, and one of the veterans.

Refreshments were served in the Parochial Hall, and we see here the Vicar and the Bishop having a cup of tea and the Bishop with a copy of Meanwood in Pictures Volume 3.

The Meanwood Men's Society always organises a family walk just after Christmas. They are seen here en route to Weardly in 2010.

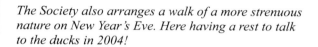

The Society also arranges a walk of a more strenuous nature on New Year's Eve. Here having a rest to talk to the ducks in 2004!

Back home in Meanwood in 2008 a case of Post Haste?

Claire and Maggie, the Meanwood Hairdressers in Greenwood Mount, having fun as they run a charity event.

Yorkshire Day celebrations at the Civic Hall in 2004. Annie Hinchcliffe, a Meanwood lady, who wrote the Yorkshire Anthem, seen in her wheelchair, attended by Christine Bewell.

The old boys of Bentley Lane school (known as the BLOBS) meet several times a year for a good lunch and a chat about the good old days. Seen here in 2002.

A group outside the Institute on Green Road in 2004. Councillor Harker, Christine Bewell, Peggy Ashton, Councillor Golton, Councillor Lancaster, Sandra Glassby, Peter Smithson, Rita Durrant, and Shirley Barber. The event was one of the very popular Sunday Pate Cheese and Plonk lunches which are organised twice a year by the Committees of the Meanwood Village Association and the Meanwood Institute.

Margaret Smithson, a happy participant.

Essential at all events, the volunteer kitchen staff, seen here at one of the 'Tea & Chat' afternoons.

Margaret Fox and Lena Sugden, the lucky raffle winners.

Freda Wilks enjoying a cuddle with Santa at a Tea and Chat afternoon at the Institute.

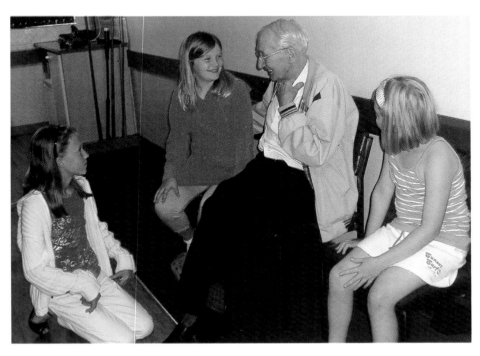

Mike Osborne, a very keen billiards and snooker player, chatting to three of his fans in the snooker room at the Institute in 2008.

In 2005 a 'Victory Party' took place in the Institute to mark the 60th anniversary of the ending of the 2nd world war. Some of the entertainment being provided by Brian Sugden, Val Milner and Jack Sykes.

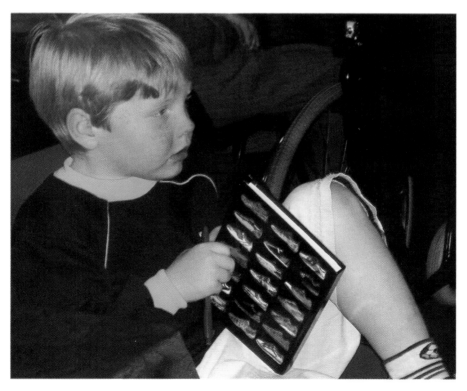

'Charlie' one of the audience.

A major development in Meanwood in 2010 was the construction of the big Waitrose store on the site of the old Capitol cinema and ballroom. The scene here shows the clearance of all the demolition rubble and the beginning of the new walls.

The start of the massive steel frame.

The steelwork in full swing.

The sign says it all.

*The entrance off
Green Road.*

The goods entrance off Monkbridge Road.

The lower level car park.

On October 25th 2011 what had been the Netto supermarket reopened under the ASDA brand and here we see the crowd all wanting to be the first in.

The big new sign.

Last minute preparations for the opening of Waitrose.

Opening day, 30th September 2010.

Mike Cooper the manager, and Councillor
Lancaster, serving mince pies on 1st December
when the Christmas lights were
being turned on.

Even Santa turned up!

It was a very snowy night, and some customers went across the road to help get the traffic
moving again.

82

Chapel Youth Club reunion at the Britannia hotel in 2008. Rita Durrant, Joyce Lister, Marjorie Hopwood, Malcolm Scholey, Shirley Richardson, Terry Richardson, Eileen Scholey, and Pat Auton.

A gathering in the chapel schoolroom to welcome back Iroko, the Japanese lady (bottom left) whom Marjorie Hopwood befriended when she lived in Meanwood.

In 2011 various events took place to mark the 200th anniversary of Methodism in Meanwood.

Rupert Weekes, the Methodist Minister, and Chris Orme, the Priest In Charge at Meanwood Parish Church, at a tea in the schoolroom following the joint Remembrance Service in 2008.

The Scouts and Cubs choir at the Christingle service in 2008.

Charles Dunbar, (1880-1960) was a master butcher in Leeds and in 1920 he became the President of the Leeds Retail Butchers Association. His daughter, Mrs Jean Maude, was delighted when the current President let her see the chain and medal, and she is seen here proudly wearing it. Some of The Dunbar family lived at Well House, a cottage opposite the well on Parkside Road, known locally as Dunny Hill. Other family members lived in Myrtle Square and at The Bay Horse.

The ornate medal.

C. DUNBAR, Esq.

40 Years Honorary Treasurer
of the Highbury Working Mens Club.

1911 — 1951

CARR MANOR SCHOOL

Opened by the Prime Minister, Tony Blair, 15th March 2007.

COMMUNITY FESTIVAL

In June 2007 a Meanwood Community Festival was held, and various events took place. This picture shows the scene outside the church following a play.

A story telling event in the garden of Ivy Cottage on Green Road.

An art exhibition in Stainbeck Church.

A gathering in Meanwoodside watching a Punch and Judy show.

VICAR'S FAREWELL PARTY

In May 2007 the Revd Richard Wiggen retired, and a party was held in the Parochial Hall to mark the occasion. Here Frances Needham bids him farewell.

Supo Ogunyinka, the Church Reader presents the Vicar's wife, Kathryn with a bouquet.

The Vicar surrounded by the church children.

It must have been a good joke!

A full house enjoying the event.

A farewell song from the choir.

Meanwood Methodist Church in 2010.

Colourful displays at the Harvest Festival in 2002.

Bringing in the haggis at the Burns night supper in the schoolroom.

The ladies in their Sunday best.

Fancy dress parade.

*A view over the tannery
dam in 2002.*

*The beck in
Meanwoodside 2003.*

*Members of the M.V.A.
outside the Institute ready
to start the traditional
Easter walk in 2003.*

Actor Christopher Timothy, a patron of the Meanwood Valley Urban Farm, seen here on a Christmas visit in 2006.

Celebrity Alan Titchmarsh at the opening of the new Courtyard Centre at the farm in 2005.

The start of a new housing development at Oddy's Fold on Parkside Road in December 2002.

Demolition of The Poplars at the top of Bentley Lane to make way for new housing in 2004.

96

**MEANWOOD PARKSIDE RD
ALLOTMENT ASSOCIATION**
FLOWER & VEGETABLE SHOW
FEATURING LIVE MUSIC
(SPONSORED BY LEEDS CITY COUNCIL)

SUNDAY 28TH AUGUST 2011
TO BE HELD AT
**THE PAROCHIAL HALL
MEMORIAL DRIVE
MEANWOOD**

OPEN TO THE PUBLIC AT 2.30 PM
AUCTION OF EXHIBITS AT 4.15 PM

ADMISSION – £1
ACCOMPANIED CHILDREN FREE

**PROFITS TO THE
HELP THE HEROES CHARITY and
YORKSHIRE AIR AMBULANCE CHARITY
£2000 RAISED LAST YEAR**

*PLEASE COME & SUPPORT US IF YOU CAN
REFRESHMENTS ON SALE*

Brenda Lancaster presenting a cup to Keith Hodgson at the Parkside Allotments show in 2011.

The publicity notice for the show.

Some of the many visitors at the show in the Parochial Hall.

The "Best in Show" cup being presented to Tony Taylor.

More of the audience.

Councillor Brenda Lancaster, the Deputy Lord Mayor, presenting a cup to Alan Lodge at the 'Launch the Wall' day in 2005.

The face painting stall.

Cynthia Ruston, the organiser, with Brenda. (Note the dry stone wall in the background).

Greg Mulholland M.P.

The Meanwood Village Association sales tent with Iain Burgess and Bryn Evans.

The Civic Trust sales tent.

THE OATES FAMILY

On March 17th 2012 it was exactly 100 years since Captain Lawrence Oates, a member of the famous Scott expedition to the South Pole, walked out of the tent to his death, after saying "I am just going outside and I may be some time." To mark this special day, various events were held in Meanwood, and over £1,000 was raised, and sent to the 'Help For Heroes' charity. The Parks Department resurfaced the car park in Meanwoodside, built a special area, and re-erected an old memorial to Edward Oates. They then fixed two information boards about Meanwoodside and a blue plaque commemorating Captain Oates.

Preparing the area.

The base of the memorial cross, with the newly gilded lettering.

The newly re-erected memorial to Edward Oates.

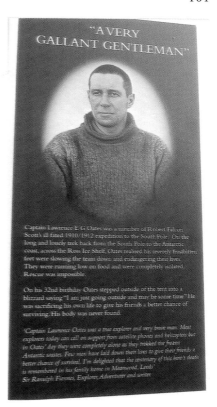

Captain Oates on the information board.

The crowd and photographers assembling for the opening ceremony.

3-2-1 – Pull! Unveiling the information boards and the blue plaque.

"A VERY GALLANT GENTLEMAN"

To commemorate
Captain Lawrence E.G. Oates
a member of Capt. Scott's expedition
to the South Pole 1910 - 1912
a frequent visitor to Meanwoodside,
the Oates family home.

Died 17th March 1912

Local M.P. Fabian Hamilton and the new plaque.

The Meanwood Institute, where various events took place on March 17th.

Meanwood C. of E. Primary School put on an excellent exhibition about Captain Oates and Antarctica, and here we see two examples.

THEN and NOW

A fascinating old postcard of the Seven Arches.
It was printed in Bavaria, posted in Leicester in 1907 and sent to an address in Germany.

The Seven Arches in January 2012. Railings in place to prevent access. (Health & safety!)

An old photograph of 44 and 46 Tannery Square with various members of the Firth family.

The same cottages in January 2012. (Now numbered 94 and 96)

*The old Becketts Arms, (originally called the Dusty Miller)
with the new 1939 building just showing on the left.*

The 1939 Becketts which was demolished in 2010.

*The latest development in 2011 consisting of several shops, and a wine bar called
"East of Arcadia" at street level, with 24 flats above.*

Batesons Tannery and cottages in Green Road, (opposite the present Waitrose).

The same site with the shops and flats above.

The current supermarket of ASDA which superseded Netto in 2011.

*Greenwood Mount in days gone by, with children playing in the traffic free road.
Note also the old gas street lamps and the local shop.*

The same road in 2011 with lots of cars. Note that many of the houses have had dormers added.

The old Capitol Parade with the well-loved cinema and ballroom and several shops. Later it became a Bingo Hall and the "Cat's Whiskers" night club before being demolished in 1980.

A supermarket (G. T. Smiths, later the Co-op) together with some shops and the Yorkshire Bank were built on the site. All were demolished in 2010.

The present Waitrose Superstore which opened in September 2010.

Brick Row, a terrace of cottages at the bottom of Church Lane. Built in 1847.

Brick Row was eventually demolished, and Church Lane Mews built on the site.

Alder Hill Cottages just off Stonegate Road. Built in 1635.

The cottages in 2011.

The shop at the bottom of Monkbridge Road, with plenty of advertisements.
For many years known as 'Gingles'.

The shop in 2011.

An old postcard showing Green Road, with Brown's grocery shop at the bottom of Church Lane.

The same place in 2011, with housing on the left and the Pet Shop on the corner.

The old cottages on Parkside Road opposite the cricket ground.
Note, some appear to have had their windows stoned up.

The cottages in 2012.

Shops at the bottom of Stonegate Road, with three ladies crossing a traffic free road.
Taken about 1913.

Websdales electrical shop which superseded the Benefit Shoe shop.

'Alfred' a wine bar now on the same site.

The public house at the junction of Meanwood Road and Grove Lane.
Officially 'The Meanwood', but known locally as 'The Melbourne'.

The pub was eventually demolished, and a block of flats built on the site.

A photograph taken in 1889 of 'Fairfax', an old house on Parkside Road which was built in 1630.

A sketch of the house made in 1904 by W. Braithwaite.

It was demolished early in the 20th century and rebuilt at right angles to the original, to face onto the road. This 2012 photograph shows the house, on the left, hidden in the trees.

Kent House, at the junction of Stonegate Road and Stainbeck Avenue. Later demolished.

The steps leading up to the Northside shopping centre are located on the site originally occupied by Kent House.

Hollin House, on the far side of Meanwood Park, with some of the Hudson family in the garden and two servants in the doorway.

The house today, which is the offices and residence of the Bishop of Ripon and Leeds.

The old Meanwood Post Office and shops at the junction of Stonegate Road and Authorpe Road.

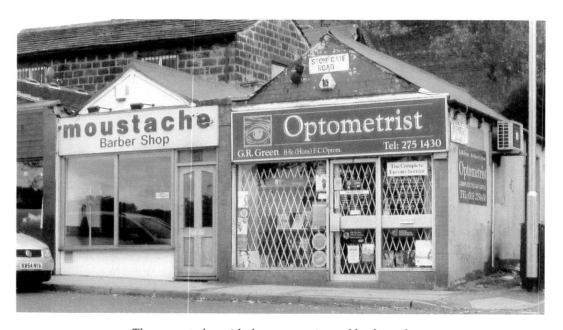

The scene today with the optometrist and barbers shops.

The War Memorial and drive up to the Church.

The site was developed into a sheltered housing scheme and named 'Memorial Drive'.

A photograph showing the old 'White Houses' at the top of Bentley Lane.

A shot from the same spot in 2011 with the present Bentley Court sheltered housing scheme. The medical centre is just off the photograph on the left.

A snowy scene at the bottom of Stainbeck Road, with more of the 'White Houses'.

The same place today with the more modern houses.

124

HISTORY IN STONES QUIZ

On the next 6 pages there are 14 photographs of datestones and rock carvings around Meanwood.
How observant are you? Try to identify them. The answers are on page 130.

A

B

C

D

E

F

G

H

I

J

K

L

M

N

OLD PHOTOGRAPHS

Location unknown, possibly Hollin House or Meanwoodside.
Caption on back states 'The Wharfedale Witches'???

1960 chapel Palm Sunday cantata.

ANSWERS TO STONES QUIZ:

A) Mystery carving on a stone boulder on the woodland path between Dunny Hill and Tongue Lane.
B) Datestone on same path.
C) Another on the same path with old and new carvings.
D) A reminder of a tragedy when Mr. Hancock shot himself on the path between Hustlers Row and Dunny Hill.
E) Over doorway at Alder Hill cottages.
F) Meanwood C. of E. School
G) On bridge over beck in Meanwoodside
H) 'Fairfax' on Parkside Road.
I) On flats at bottom of Church Lane (Formerly Acorn Glass).
J) High up over Marcel's at terminus.
K) Stone pillar in field adjacent Stonegate Road.
L) Cottage on Meanwood Grove.
M) On the old tannery (Highbury Works).
N) On Cottage on Parkside Road.

The Methodist Sunday School Carnival Queen (Susan Siddaway) with her attendants in 1965.

4 girls on their way to the carnival in the 1960s.

The Methodist Minister, Alan Powers, with his wife Sheila, son Conrad, Kathryn Smith, Angela King, ? , and ? at the Chapel anniversary in 1979.

The Slabbering Baby spring near the old Verity's tea rooms at Adel.

A fossilised tree in the ganister stone beds.

What are thought to be Celtic stone heads discovered near Carr Manor.

A similar head which is built into an interior wall in Alder Hill Cottages.
Could the slabbering baby head be from the same source?

134

Children of Bentley Lane School in about 1931. Including Jim Forsyth, Andrew McArthur, Geoffrey Silburn, Maurice Dales, David Mann, Bryan Wyatt, Kenneth Sheard, Kenneth Storr, Alan Oxlee, Joan Wilkinson, Doreen Rogers, Marjorie Barret, Esme Nettleton, Jimmy Stahope, Kenneth Halton, and Leo Waters.

Members of the uniformed organisations forming up outside the Methodist Church ready to go on the monthly parade around Meanwood.

Children in Bentley Lane School in 1938. Raymond Hawkshaw in centre of left row.

The original Yorkshire Bank. The site now occupied by Ladbrokes betting shop.

The building at the top of the Highburys which was used in the 1940s as an annexe of Bentley Lane School, and also by the Methodist cubs when the Chapel schoolroom was being used for the making of camouflage nets in the early days of the war.

*An interesting cartoon of
'Riding the Stang' an old
West Riding custom. In cases
of marital quarrels leading
to wife beating, the culprit
or his effigy was subjected to
the ignomy of being tied to a
stang (a pole or beam) and
carried shoulder high round
the village, accompanied by
jeering mobs drumming on
old cans and pans.*

*A tram opposite the Woodhouse cricket ground in Meanwood Road in 1955.
Two important Meanwood employers can be seen in the background. Bullus Dyeworks
and the Yorkshire Switchgear.*

A group of ladies in fancy dress in the grounds of Meanwoodside or Hollin House.

Martha Lynch (nee Oddy) and Gertrude Lynch in this fine old photograph taken in the late 1800s.

Two cartoons about the Bay Horse Bowling Club in 1918.

141

When the whole blamed world is upside down,
And business on the " bum,"
A two cent grin and a lifted chin
Helps some, my boy, helps some !

With best wishes from

the President (George F. Warden)

for a Happy Christmas
and
a Bright and Prosperous New Year.

1, Wilton Grove,
   Headingley, Leeds.   Christmas, 1920.

A message from the President in 1920.

A wintry scene of the bowling green at the back of the Bay Horse.

An old shot of the much talked about 'Revolution Well' in Stonegate Road.

The inscription on the Well

Pearson's off licence shop in Green Road, also known as 'Taddys',
prior to being demolished about 1960.

Myrtle Square with an old car.

Housing and shop in Tannery Square on Green
Road just prior to demolition.

A nice rural scene to end with. Haymaking the old fashioned way with King Alfred's castle in the background.